SUMMARY: EDUCATED

A MEMOIR BY TARA WESTOVER

EXECUTIVEGROWTH
SUMMARIES

For those who dare ask more, learn more, and become more.

TABLE OF CONTENTS

BACKGROUND & GROWTH POTENTIAL

In *Educated: A Memoir*, Dr. Tara Westover recounts her experiences growing up at the base of rural Idaho's Buck's Peak mountain under the authority of fundamentalist Mormon parents and an abusive older brother. Her father believed public education to be a danger to their way of life, and therefore Tara did not attend school. Her mother, a self-taught midwife and herbalist, served as the family's source of medical assistance during illnesses and even for severe injuries resulting from vehicle accidents and working with their father in the family junkyard.

Tara eventually left her mountain home and received a formal education, graduating *magna cum laude* from Brigham Young University and then earning her PhD from Cambridge University while also winning a Gates Cambridge Scholarship. The process of becoming educated set her on a path that proved unacceptable to her parents, several of her six siblings, and other family members.

It was also a path that gave Tara the ability to perceive her entire childhood in a much different light. In that light, she found a truer way of existing.

Tara's book has received much praise from credible sources. In addition to being on President Barack Obama's recommended reading list …

"Alluring … courageous."
— NEW YORK TIMES

★★★★ out of four
"A heartbreaking, heartwarming, best-in-years memoir."
— USA TODAY

"Beautiful and propulsive."
— VOGUE

"An amazing story, and truly inspiring. It's even better than you've heard."
— BILL GATES

"Superb."
— THE TIMES

"Fit to stand alongside the great modern memoirs."
— THE SUNDAY TIMES

"Westover writes with uncommon intelligence and grace."
— NEWSDAY

"A transformation so courageous, so entire, as to beggar belief."
— FINANCIAL TIMES

"A one-of-a-kind memoir."
— THE ATLANTIC

"Fascinating … extraordinarily evocative."
— THE IRISH TIMES

"One of the most talked-about and critically acclaimed books of the year."
— PBS NEWSHOUR/NYTIMES BOOK CLUB

POWER INSIGHTS

As our valued reader, you are important to us. We cherish your time and focus. When reading the following **Power Insights** you will instantly capture key takeaways from *Educated*, create an effective mental map of the book, and be able to better retain the remainder of the summary.

* * *

The extreme nature of Tara's parents' lifestyle is revealed in Tara's retelling of specific instances from her childhood and young adult life. Some of these will be shared throughout this e-book, but it is important that you, the reader, have a general overview of Tara's story before delving in further.

Tara's father believed his faith required him and his family to live "off the grid," without interaction or reliance on hospitals, public education, utilities, or governmental entities. He stockpiled weapons by burying them around his property. He constantly warned his children about the coming End of Days and explained how they would be the only ones with electricity, water, and food because of all his planning. To earn money, her dad operated a junkyard, crushing cars and mining old machinery for metal that could be salvaged and sold. He also took various construction jobs in the area. He focused on working quickly rather than safely and held the highest regard for his own opinion. This often resulted in his children getting injured while working with him; burns, brain injuries, cuts, bruises, and broken bones were a way of life for the family.

He and his wife claim to have "homeschooled" their children. Tara's account, however, shows little systematic or purpose-driven education in the home. She and two of her siblings, at the objection of her dad, left and received their formal education up to and including PhDs.

One of Tara's older brothers, Shawn, was physically, mentally, and verbally abusive to her and others. Tara's parents did nothing to stop this.

Their faith dictated that Tara's father was the leader of the family. His decisions and direction were final. Tara's mother modeled submission and subservience to her husband for the rest of the family. The father's willful ignorance on any matter he deemed "sinful" or a temptation away from their faith led to many instances of pain for the entire family and, sometimes, for himself.

Because he saw hospitals and doctors as tools of the devil/government and sinful to be used, Tara's dad did not bring his children to sources of modern medicine to find treatment for their various injuries. Instead, he relied on his wife, Tara's mother, to heal every ailment homeopathically. For example, when he accidentally set himself on fire while crushing cars, Tara's father refused to be taken to the hospital. Instead, Tara's mother treated him with her homemade salves and tinctures. While he lived, he was left scarred, lacking lips and some of his face. From treating extensive burns to head trauma and more, Tara's mother eventually built an expansive personal knowledge of, and experience with, various herbs, plants, and essential oils to address her family's—and their like-minded friends'—health needs. That ultimately became the thriving natural medicine business her mother and father run today.

The home life in which Tara was raised constantly warred with Tara's innate and growing awareness that something wasn't right, that she should be going about life differently. As that awareness came to fruition, so, too, did the point at which she had to decide between an educated life and a life with her parents. Her parents would not allow for both.

Throughout the course of this book, we will mine some of the memories and situations Tara shared in order to uncover nine life principles that can be useful for nearly any life path:

1. Choices Create Outcomes

2. When Your Present Costs Too Much, You'll Seek a New Situation

3. If You Don't Know Better, You'll Accept Less Than What's Possible

4. Your Perception Changes When Your Input Changes

5. Age-Old Authority Sources Aren't Always Wiser Than You Are

6. Failing or Succeeding in the Growth Space Tempts You Back Toward the Familiar

7. Old Ways May Hinder You in the Growth Space

8. You'll Lie to Yourself Rather than Let Truth Grow You

9. Setting Your Past in Its Proper Place Begets Freedom

These ideas become clear and applicable as we lay them upon the backdrop of Tara's experiences.

* * *

If you enjoyed the **Power Insights** and want to keep a copy as a reference or to share with your friends and family members, feel free to download your exclusive digital copy by following the web address: https://www.exegrowth.com/pdfguide-e-20

You can also follow the steps below to instantly access your exclusive Power Insights guide:

1. **Open** your smart phone's camera application

2. **Aim** your phone's camera **and focus on** the QR Code below

3. **Click** the link that pops up on the top side of your screen

Now get ready to uncover a new understanding of yourself, your past, and your truth that very few hold.

SUMMARY CHAPTERS

CHAPTER 1:
CHOICES CREATE OUTCOMES

Several passages from *Educated* illustrate the principle that Choices Create Outcomes. Let's look at three.

The first is Tara's grandmother's account of the legend of Apache tears. Her grandmother takes Tara and her brother Luke up the mountain and, after showing them two examples pulled from within her own pockets, instructs the children to go gather certain black rocks around a sediment formation. Luke recognizes the stones as obsidian. On their way back down the mountain, Grandma shares that about 100 years ago the site they just visited was the scene of a battle between the U.S. Cavalry and a tribe of Apaches. When the Apache men realized they were going to lose the battle, they rode their horses off the cliff rather than be taken prisoner. Upon finding their broken bodies, the Apache women cried tears that turned to stone when they landed on the earth. Those stones were the black ones just retrieved by the children that Grandma would now sell.

Tara reflected on how the choices of the Apache men set the course for the Apache women, who likely became slaves of the Cavalry.

Long before the moment in which the men flung themselves off the cliff, they'd decided to be "warriors" as defined by their tribe. "Long before the warriors' leap it was decided how the women would live and how they would die," Tara wrote. Those choices changed the course of the women's lives and, mythically, led to the formation of stone that the children had just visited.

Next, in Chapter 2, we see Tara's mother providing the local midwife with homeopathic medicines and tinctures made from calendula, witch hazel, and lobelia. Her mother is intimidated by the midwife but even more so by Tara's father, who is adamant that his wife become a midwife. He couches his opinion as a calling of the Lord on Tara's mother. "And sometimes the Lord asks for hard things."

Tara sees her dad's demand on her mother as fueling his desire to be self-reliant. Tara's mother can earn money as a midwife and help others avoid hospitals and modern medicine.

Tara's mother becoming a midwife helped set the course for the thriving holistic medicine business that she and her husband run today—a business that appears to generate far more earnings than Tara's dad ever did with his various junkyard and building endeavors. We can see here again that choices created outcomes years later. Tara's mom chose to marry her dad. That choice, according to their religion, put her in a position of succumbing to his authority and choices for her life. His choice for his wife to become a midwife ultimately ends up providing the ability for the family to have the lifestyle to which her husband aspires.

Our third example is of a more immediate outcome resulting from choices and is shared in Chapter 4. It begins with Tara's mother deciding the family needs a trip to the Arizona home of her husband's parents, with the hope that this will alleviate her husband's current depression. (Tara suggests later that it's possible her dad suffers from bipolar disorder, a condition she learns about after leaving the family home and attending college.) The trip seems to work and her dad, now back to his decisive ways, announces it's time they head back home. The only problem is that it's early evening and he's the only one who thinks it's wise to leave at that hour to complete a 12-hour drive.

Her mom's choice to go on the trip and her dad's choice to end it abruptly lead to a car accident. Tara's mother suffers a debilitating brain injury that affects her memory, brings on near-constant pain, and yet ultimately leads to the growth of her mother and father's reliance on homeopathic remedies for even the most severe injuries.

There is a temptation in this principle to play the "What if?" game. What if her mother hadn't decided to go to Arizona? What if her dad had been more reasonable in choosing a departure time? What if her brother, Tyler, hadn't fallen asleep at the wheel? Would things have worked out differently for the entire family? Would her mother have still eventually become the success she is today in natural medicine?

But to ask these questions is to miss the point of the principle. The point is that those choices *did* create outcomes. In considering the

CHAPTER 2:
WHEN YOUR PRESENT COSTS TOO MUCH, YOU'LL SEEK A NEW SITUATION (AND FIND A NEW VALUABLE THING)

We've all been there: caught in a situation we do not like or want, but which isn't bad enough to leave. Three examples from *Educated* remind us that, at the point at which your present costs more than you're willing to give, you will seek a new situation. And, in seeking a new situation, you may often find a new, more valuable circumstance.

Tara has begun to realize that she does not want the life she's being forced to lead—a life that doesn't allow her to go to school and requires that she put herself in harm's way to obey her dad's commands in their junkyard. And yet Tara makes no move to change her situation until the day her leg is ripped open by a piece of scrap metal. She's 10 years old, and her dad instructs Tara to climb into a bin filled with scrap metal. He explains that he will operate a forklift to lift the bin, with Tara inside it, over to a trailer. She is to jump into the trailer, move to the side of the trailer and wait for the forklift to dump the metal contents of the bin into the center of the trailer. Then she is to settle the scrap metal to condense the trailer load, making more room for the next pile of dropped metal. Tara at first balks. This feels dangerous. But her dad is insistent that this is the most efficient way, and so Tara does as she's told.

The metal shifts when her dad begins moving the bin, and a jagged piece catches on Tara's leg, slicing it open. Her dad can't see that Tara is now pinned to the bin. She can't jump out before he flips the bin and dumps the contents into the trailer. She's scared she'll be powerfully tossed, falling on hundreds of edges of metal as even more rain down on her. As the metal shifts, it gashes deeply into her leg but finally releases her. In a quick decision, Tara throws herself over the side of the bin, falling hard to the ground instead of into the trailer with all the jagged metal.

It takes her until the wound has closed over in a dark and shiny scab, "a black river flowing through pink flesh," before Tara comes to the place where her present costs too much to continue within it. She stands before her dad and announces, "I want to go to school."

Yet, in hearing this, her dad places another, higher price to pay at Tara's feet. He references a Bible story that communicates to Tara the cost of her going to school: he equates her desire to attend public school with selling out her faith, her relationship with God.

Faced with this new cost, Tara backs down.

Tara shares other instances when she could have decided that some particular abuse by her dad or her brother Shawn reached the deciding line: the cost that went too far and would propel her out of her dad's way of life/faith into a different way. She repeatedly backs down until the day she comes upon Shawn's motorcycle wreck.

People have gathered at the scene. Shawn is lying in a pool of his own blood. Tara rushes to stop the bleeding and believes she can see bits of his brain in the cuts. She calls her dad, who tells Tara to bring Shawn home and have their mother treat him with her homeopathic treatments.

Tara is torn. Shawn has already suffered a brain injury from another accident working with their father. He nearly died then because their dad didn't get medical attention at the time—and he has been mentally altered ever since. His rages have led to physical harm for Tara and other people. The cost of her brother's life is too high for Tara to risk. She takes Shawn to the hospital.

At the hospital a CAT scan reveals the damage is minimal, although the wound is bad. By this time her father has come to the hospital, and they end up taking Shawn home. On the car ride, Tara can tell that something has shifted between her and her dad. Because she chose modern medicine for Shawn, because she completely disobeyed her dad's order to bring Shawn home to her mother for treatment, a line has been drawn. "After that night, there was never any question of whether I would go or stay," she writes regarding the decision to leave for school. "It was as if we were living in the future, and I was already gone."

This example illustrates that, at the point at which staying the course will cost Tara a price she refuses to pay, she alters the trajectory.

The ultimate example of this principle comes at the end of *Educated*. At this point, Tara has walked an increasingly taut line between her educated worlds of Harvard and Cambridge University and the uneducated family life on the mountain. She's begun admitting aloud the physical and emotional abuse that Shawn has heaped on her. She's aware, now, of the harmful nature of her dad's way of life and choices.

Her parents come to visit her at Harvard, and her dad "testifies" that she's been seduced by the devil. By continuing on this path of receiving an education and openly acknowledging the abuse she suffered at the hands of her brother, he claims, she is becoming a tool of the devil's evil plans.

Her parents force Tara to choose between her new life of education and awareness or her family's way of life.

Tara now has acquired the clarity to truly assess the cost of the choice before her. As with the time she chose to take Shawn to the hospital rather than rely on her mother's homeopathic treatment alone, Tara calculates the cost of her dad's ways to be too high. And this, in turn, allows her to choose a new way.

This can be true in your life as well. Whether it is a job, relationship, physical situation, or something else, you may find yourself in a place where the maintenance of your present way costs more than you're willing to give. At that point, you'll find a new way.

And, as Tara learned, you may find a whole new world out there that you had no idea even existed.

CHAPTER 3:
IF YOU DON'T KNOW BETTER, YOU'LL ACCEPT LESS THAN WHAT'S POSSIBLE (AKA IGNORANCE ALLOWS ABUSE)

Tara's entire life experience is an example of this principle, but let's look at a few instances in particular.

First, Tara's experience breaking horses alongside her brother Shawn illustrates that if you don't know anything better, you'll accept less than what's possible. Often, she and Shawn try to break feral horses—horses that have known only a wild life of freedom on the mountain. She never succeeds. The horses know what they'll be giving up, and not one of them succumbs to Tara's attempts to break them.

Then one day Tara and Shawn are presented with the opportunity to break a horse she calls The Yearling.

After many hours in the ring, Shawn manages to get a saddle on The Yearling. He slides up into the saddle and, in a move that surprises Tara, The Yearling acquiesces. His hooves come off the ground as if he's considering the act of bucking, but just as quickly the horse's feet come back down and the animal settles into this new life situation.

Tara writes, "He had never been feral, so he could not hear the maddening call of that *other* world, on the mountain, in which he could not be owned, could not be ridden."

In other words, the horse didn't know any better than what he was being forced to do, so he did it.

Another example comes in Chapter 23 of *Educated*. At 15 years old, Tara has begun wearing lip gloss and mascara. She is also regularly experiencing physical abuse at Shawn's hands and mental abuse as he calls her "whore" and manipulates her emotionally. One day Shawn tells their father that he has heard rumors in town that Tara has a "reputation." Her dad yells at her mother, claiming Tara is pregnant and attributing this development to letting Tara perform in some plays in town. Her mother maintains that Tara is trustworthy. But Shawn, coming from his twisted experience with girls, counters that no girl is trustworthy—and the ones who seem religiously faithful are the worst.

Tara sits in her room listening to this, honestly wondering if she is pregnant. She stands before her mirror and runs her hand over her belly, thinking about whether a baby is growing inside her.

In reality, she has never even kissed a boy.

Telling the reader about this experience, Tara concludes that the "whore" accusation was more of an attack on someone's essence than a label based on actions. She had given Shawn the power to label her. "He had defined me to myself, and there's no greater power than that," she writes.

But someone can't define you to yourself if you know what the words really mean and who you really are. Tara lacked both of those pieces of information at that point in her life. Her ignorance allowed for her abuse, though it by no means excuses such.

A final example to consider is one Tara experiences during her time at Brigham Young University. She has a fractured tooth and wakes to blinding pain in her jaw. She does not, however, have the money to get the tooth fixed. The situation becomes known to her bishop, who kindly offers money to Tara to get her tooth fixed.

But Tara has been raised by a man who sees self-reliance as righteous. Take money from people and they'll own you, he believes. This is so ingrained in Tara that she refuses the bishop's offer of money and instead suffers. This is a stark example of ignorance allowing your own harm.

The bishop is there *to help the students*. By allowing her father's ignorant ways to govern her actions, Tara welcomes physical pain and suffering into her life that could have been swiftly alleviated.

What is causing pain in your life right now? Could it be hurting you because you don't yet know a better way? Or are you like the feral horses, having tasted a certain way and being unwilling to

CHAPTER 4: PERCEPTION CHANGES WHEN INPUT CHANGES

This feels like an obvious idea, doesn't it? If someone tells you for your entire life that the sky is green, you will always believe it to be green—until someone informs you about the color blue.

Tara grows up, metaphorically speaking, hearing that the sky was green. And yet her brother, Tyler, leaves the mountain and begins to see the myriad colors present in the world. He comes back one day and, as luck or fate would have it, happens to be present during one of Shawn's outbursts of beating and berating Tara. While Tara lies on the kitchen floor seeing the spots before her eyes that hint of a blessed coming unconsciousness, Tyler comes up the stairs in the hallway. Before him, his brother Shawn holds his sister Tara in a stronghold—one hand keeping her wrist wrenched behind her back and the other hand on her throat. This is a familiar posture to Tara by now. She's already gone in her mind to what she knows will come in a day or so: Shawn at her bedside, apologizing.

And yet this time the script changes. This time, Tyler comes into the room and provides Tara with an escape: his truck keys. Tara runs.

She does, though, return. And the scene plays out as she'd anticipated. Soon Shawn was in her room, apologizing.

But this time Tyler changes Tara's input. He sits with her on the couch and says, "It's time to go, Tara. The longer you stay, the less likely you will ever leave." He encourages Tara to take the ACT and apply to Brigham Young University. She can tell the admissions officers she was homeschooled, although their education at home has been nearly non-existent.

This new input breaks the loop of Tara's thinking and life experience. Before this, the cycle of Shawn going into a rage, harming Tara, apologizing to Tara and then being kind to Tara kept repeating. Now, Tyler provides new input: an alternative way.

Tara begins studying for the ACT.

She comes up against a kind of math that neither she nor her mother can fathom, and this provides a keen observation worth considering. At her mother's suggestion, Tara takes the issue to her dad. He quickly works out the solution to the problems, but he cannot explain to Tara how he arrived at the answer. Tara observes, "Dad could command this science, could decipher its language, decrypt its logic, could bend and twist and squeeze from it the truth. But as it passed through him, it turned to chaos."

This is wise insight into the power of input. Her father had received enough instruction and education to arrive at a proper output, but he could not pass along the necessary information—he couldn't *input* it into another—for the ability to pass on to a new generation. Consider that principle. Is it present in your life?

A second instance of the power of changed input happens in Chapter 20. At this point, Tara has begun receiving a formal education at BYU. Her eyes are opening to the breadth of historical information unknown to her (e.g. she did not have a proper understanding of the Holocaust). During a visit home, Shawn welcomes Tara by saying, "Our nigger's back!"

Shawn has called Tara many names over the course of her life, including that one. Because she had never been taught its history and cultural context, though, she'd never been offended by it. But this time is different. Now, Tara had received input. She'd learned of Martin Luther King, Jr., of Rosa Parks, of Emmett Till. When she realized that her mother was four years old when Emmett was killed, history came off the book pages and stepped into her as real, flesh-and-blood, life. The input of images and words opened Tara's eyes to a broader awareness and appreciation of the Civil Rights Movement.

Now, when Shawn greets Tara by calling her a nigger, the word falls upon ears that immediately place it into full cultural and historical context—and she cringes. "Don't call me that," she says to Shawn. "You don't know what it means."

In his ignorance, Shawn replies, "Sure I do. You've got black all over your face, like a nigger."

What a stark example of the power of input to temper us into individuals who can move through the world without harming our fellow humans. Tara writes of her awakening by saying, "I had begun to understand that we had lent our voices to a discourse whose sole purpose was to dehumanize and brutalize others—because nurturing that discourse was easier, because retaining power always *feels* like the way forward."

While Shawn meant the word in the same way he always had—simple name-calling—Tara now recognized it for what it is. "Never again," she vowed, "would I allow myself to be made a foot soldier in a conflict I did not understand."

That vow comes into play in a different way in Chapter 32 and provides a third illustration of the power of input to change perception. Tara has just been accepted into Cambridge's PhD program when her mom calls to tell her that "Grandma-down-the-hill" (Tara's dad's mom) is very sick and Tara should come home. Tara arrives home to find her house a buzz of activity. Her mother's homeopathic treatments business has exploded. People are everywhere, filling bottles with tinctures, seeking out her mother for medical advice, and placing orders. Her dad is snatching up the ever-ringing phone, affirming to the callers that "the Lord" can cure what ails them.

And then Grandma-down-the-hill dies. The house grows quiet. It's just the family now. Her mom wants her dad to help write the thank-you cards to everyone who sent flowers and food. Her dad refuses, seeing it as "wifely work." For the first time, Tara hears her mother refuse to do what her dad is demanding. Instead, her mother—now the head of a successful business and the clear breadwinner in the home—finds a voice to tell him if he expects her to do the wifely work then he should do the husband's work (be the breadwinner).

The next morning, Tara finds her dad in the kitchen making a poor attempt at putting together pancake batter. Upon seeing Tara, he drops the flour, sits down, and tells her, "You're a woman, ain'tcha? Well, this here's a kitchen."

Tara suddenly sees the distance that now separates them as those words are quite natural to her father and yet grating to her educated ears.

This is a powerful example of the power of input to change not only perception, but also self-worth, purpose, and behavior. Before leaving her mountain home, Tara knew a woman's place only as in service to her husband and children. Now, she knows that there are many other options—and, further, that her own father hasn't shared any such options or input with her. This new input allows Tara to see her father's words in a much different light—dare we say, an empowering light?

Input matters. The information you allow into your mind changes how you observe and interact with your life. It can alter your entire journey.

It did for Tara.

CHAPTER 5:
AGE-OLD AUTHORITY SOURCES AREN'T ALWAYS WISER THAN YOU ARE

As we saw in the previous chapter, the age-old authority sources aren't always wiser than the new information you've received. Tara's family religion and her father would have her primary purpose be in subservience to a future husband and children—as shown by her father expecting her to cook for him just because she was the female and he the male.

Her dad often used the age-old sources of Bible and faith tradition to enforce certain behaviors and ideas from Tara.

One spring before Tara has managed to score well on the ACT and go off to college, her father calls her into the junkyard to work with him. Her teenage body has blossomed into young womanhood and she has already endured numerous verbal and physical assaults by her brother Shawn, who routinely calls her a whore, slut, or bitch and tells their parents she has a reputation in town. (She does not.)

In the scorching sun, Tara's brother Luke tears the sleeves from his shirt in order to allow some air circulation. They're hauling purlins (iron beams that run horizontally along a roof) and are overheating. Tara won't dare tear her own sleeves off, but she does roll them up to just past her shoulders.

Her dad sees this and yanks the sleeves back down. "This ain't a whorehouse," he tells her and walks away. Pouring sweat, she rolls them back up. An hour later, he sees what she has done and yanks both sleeves back down. She again rolls them up.

And it occurs to her that, covered as she is in grime and dirt that will take a half-hour that night to dig out of her nostrils and ears, she does not feel like an object of desire or temptation. In that moment, it makes no sense to Tara that she can't roll up her sleeves and be a bit more comfortable while doing her job.

Tara is beginning to see that the age-old authority's idea that she is, at all times and in all ways, first an object of sexual temptation to be avoided and covered up does not jive with reality.

This and other instances of her dad's "voice of authority" not resonating with Tara after she comes to know truths via her own life experience that cause her to shift further and further away from blind acceptance of age-old authority. Ultimately, she will have to let go of an overarching lesson her father taught, that "there are not two reasonable opinions to be had on any subject: there is Truth and there are Lies."

Tara came to learn the lie in that position. In truth, there can be many reasonable opinions on any given subject. Accepting this and learning to live at peace with it is paramount.

CHAPTER 6:
FAILING IN THE GROWTH SPACE TEMPTS YOU BACK TOWARD THE FAMILIAR

Doing a new thing is hard, isn't it? It isn't just that what you approach is an unknown, which doesn't allow you to prepare for all the possibilities and hold off potential failure or harm—it's that you have to *step out of your comfort space* to do the new thing.

Comfort may mean actual physical or mental comfort, or it may just mean *that which is familiar*. Familiarity breeds comfort because you know where your walls and protections need to be.

If there is anything that Tara Westover struggles with, it is the siren call of the familiar. She earnestly wishes to return to it, to be accepted within it, to be approved of within it, even while her own identity grows farther and farther beyond its bounds.

Her honest sharing of the struggle lets us contemplate with her the hows and whys of going back to the familiar. On the surface, we could easily wonder why Tara keeps returning to a place where she is often physically, mentally, and verbally abused. Once you break free, how can anything lure you back?

The chase of parental approval. The longing to be accepted by your family. The need to be known by those you love and know. To be seen.

All of that and more.

Each time you experience failure (or even, sometimes, success) in your growth space, you may be tempted—like Tara—to go back to the familiar. Better to stay with the harm you know than the devil you don't, right? As Tara's life shows us: wrong.

When Tara first tries to take the ACT, she walks into a classroom at Utah State University and sits down at a desk amidst other students. The test proctor places a sheet on her desk. It is filled with answer "bubbles." Tara has never seen such a thing and asks what it is. The proctor explains it is a bubble sheet on which she will record her answers. Tara has to ask how it works. The proctor just looks at Tara for a minute before explaining.

Tara goes on to take the ACT in that white classroom filled with unfamiliar noises—the rustle of turning pages, the scratch of pencils on paper—and leaves feeling stupid and ridiculous.

She stepped out of her familiar into a growth space and failed. That failure sends her running back to a familiar place, donning her overalls and stepping back into working for her dad even though this has caused her physical harm.

Later, Tara recounts taking her first quiz at BYU. She'd tried to read the required materials, but so many unfamiliar terms—like "civic humanism" and "Scottish enlightenment"—confused her ignorant ears that she could make neither heads nor tails of the information. She completely failed the quiz. It is enlightening to read about her take on this:

"My loyalty to my father had increased in proportion to the miles between us. On the mountain, I could rebel. But here, in this loud, bright place, surrounded by gentiles disguised as saints, I clung to every truth, every doctrine he had given me. Doctors were Sons of Perdition. Homeschooling was a commandment from the Lord."

See how quickly a failure pushes Tara back to her familiar? And yet she *is* growing beyond its bounds whether she fully recognizes it yet or not.

In her next class, she is exposed to art. One specific piece's description includes the word "Holocaust." This is not a word Tara knows. When she asks the teacher for its meaning, the entire class falls silent. The teacher, after a pause, only says, "Thanks for *that*." He doesn't realize she's asking an honest question.

But Tara realizes it is a question that, if her familiar were correct, she would have no need of asking. This gives Tara some freedom to question her familiar and choose her journey into growth.

When you are tempted to return to a place of abuse and dead ends, solely because it is *familiar*, think of one concrete instance where you solidly knew that the familiar place did not serve you well.

For Tara, it was in that day of realizing she did not know about the Holocaust. Having a stark example of how poorly her familiar space had prepared her for life helped Tara to keep walking away from the familiar space.

What can help you walk away from yours?

CHAPTER 7:
OLD WAYS MAY HINDER YOU
IN THE NEW SPACE

When you attempt to enter into a new space, or grow into a better way of being, your old ways could be a significant hindrance. We find four illustrations of this principle in *Educated*.

In Chapter 17, we find Tara earnestly trying to make a go of it at Brigham Young University. As you've probably assessed, nothing in Tara's life prepared her for the experience of formal education. Further, the acceptable behaviors of her old life are proving to be a hindrance in this new space. Case in point: resting on the Sabbath.

Tara really wants to respect and observe the requirement that her father has said is part of their faith: to rest on the Sabbath. Her roommates let Tara know that this will not work well with the BYU study load. Tara, though, tries mightily to abide by her old way in this new setting. She observes that the other students— who also profess to believe in her faith tradition—*do* study on the Sabbath and go to movies on the Sabbath. They even wear skirts above the knee! And they all seem to be succeeding in their education.

"I understood now," Tara writes, "I could stand with my family, or with the gentiles, on the one side or the other, but there was no foothold in between."

A second example lies early in Tara's childhood, when her brother Luke comes across a great horned owl in their pasture. The bird is unconscious and half frozen. Luke brings it home, and their mother does what she can to treat a wound caused by a thorn. As days pass and the owl heals, it begins thrashing about the kitchen—harming itself and causing destruction in an effort to return to the way of life it knows best. As Tara writes, "It didn't belong. It couldn't be taught to belong." The owl had its ways *and showed no sign of embracing new ways to thrive in its new environment*. As a result, it could only find and cause harm in a new environment.

Conversely, when Tara learns that Bob Marley—the man who said, "Emancipate yourselves from mental slavery"—died from a melanoma that, but for Marley's faith's prohibition on modern medicine, could have been easily treated, her awakening grows. She's already learned that strict adherence to resting on the Sabbath doesn't work in this new space. The prohibition on engaging in modern medicine was also something her father and faith decreed. And yet here Tara is faced with its outcome: the preventable death of a talented and otherwise insightful man. Tara is not the owl thrashing about in the kitchen, needing to return to her old environment. She is becoming a new creature, open to learning new ways.

She writes, "…although I had renounced my father's world, I had never quite found the courage to live in this one." In that moment, though, Tara does find the courage. She writes in her notebook, "None but ourselves can free our minds." Then she picks up the phone and makes an appointment to get her vaccinations.

See, Tara didn't just walk into a new world filled with completely foreign behaviors and beliefs, toting her old ways alongside. No. She walked in *and began taking that world into herself*. She learned about it, studied it, deliberated its differences with her upbringing, and then made a conscious choice to adopt what she believed was best.

When you come into the new space, the growth space, consider whether you are bringing your old ways into it and whether/how they work in this new space. Growth might require you to set aside old ways and embrace new, better ones.

CHAPTER 8:
YOU'LL LIE TO YOURSELF RATHER THAN LET TRUTH GROW YOU

As Tara progresses in her education and maturation, she often struggles with the pain that a newly learned truth causes. There is a temptation to sit in the comforting familiarity of a lie rather than breathe through the fire of truth that burns it away. For Tara, this temptation often comes about in her relationships.

As teenagers, Tara and a young man named Charles begin developing a romantic relationship. Eventually, Charles comes to Tara's home for dinner. The evening devolves into Shawn's customary physical and verbal attacks on Tara: calling her names, wrenching her wrist behind her back and pushing her face into the floor. When Tara's apology is spoken only as a whisper (she doesn't want Charles to hear her), Shawn escalates and yanks Tara to her feet by grabbing a fistful of her hair and pulling. He drags her down the hallway to the bathroom and—not for the first time—shoves her head into the toilet. Tara fights back, desperate for Charles not to see her like this. She gets one foot into the hallway, but Shawn grabs her hair again and pulls her back so hard they both tumble into the bathtub. Her toe breaks.

Charles continually asks Tara, "Are you okay?" and Tara retreats to the familiar lie. She assures Charles she's fine. Charles leaves. They meet up later—not at the house—and Charles again gives Tara an opportunity to come into the truth of her family and life.

But Tara isn't ready. "What *was* important to me wasn't love or friendship," she writes, "but my ability to lie convincingly to myself: to believe I was strong. I could never forgive Charles for knowing I wasn't."

Tara isn't lying only to Charles. She lies to herself for years, making up excuses for Shawn's behavior and rewriting the reality in her head to fit a story that would be acceptable. She even goes so far as to see *herself* as the problem, not Shawn. "It's comforting to think the defect is mine, because that means it is under my power."

Tara hasn't yet learned that accepting a lie won't give her the control over her chaotic life that she seeks. Accepting the *truth* will.

Living in the lie turns Tara into someone who is more comfortable with cruelty than kindness. When her first essay at Cambridge draws abject praise from Professor Steinberg, Tara's reaction is exactly as it was that night in Charles's Jeep when he put a kind hand over hers and asked if she was okay. Tara runs. Her acceptance of violence and the lies she's told herself *about herself* to make them okay have stolen Tara's ability to see herself as worthy of a kind word or touch from another person.

Through her education, Tara continues to mature and allow truth to grow her. She receives an email from her sister, Audrey, asking if she will join Audrey in talking with their parents about Shawn's abuse of them both. Later, Tara has an online chat conversation with her mother wherein her mother acknowledges that her dad is bipolar and that Shawn abused Tara. Her mother apologizes for not protecting Tara and leads to Tara to believe that she and Tara's father are going to get Shawn help.

On a subsequent trip to visit them, Tara has a conversation with Shawn wherein Shawn asks Tara if she's been talking with Audrey. He tells Tara, "I'd put a bullet in her head, but I don't want to waste a good bullet on a worthless bitch."

Tara shares the threat with her parents. Her father's immediate defense of Shawn reveals to Tara that her mother has not discussed this with her father as she'd indicated she would. Further, Shawn's abuse and rage have not been addressed. Shawn is called to the house and shows Tara a short knife with blood on it. She later learns that, when her parents called Shawn to come over for the discussion, Shawn went outside his trailer and killed his son's dog with a short knife while his son listened to the dog's cries.

The scene is a particularly brutal one in an already hard life story. Tara yo-yos between her old, unfeeling/encased self and her new self that has begun accepting kindness and tenderness. This time, though, she won't let the lie live within her. Though she delivers the expected words and behaviors to her family, she knows them now as false. She is putting on an act so that she can get out of the

CHAPTER 9:
SETTING YOUR PAST INTO ITS PROPER PLACE BRINGS FREEDOM

Walking away from old ways and into new ones doesn't eradicate the old life. As we've seen here, the experiences in your new space may even push you back into your old space. Tara's journey leads her to finally set her past into its proper place. Doing so gives Tara freedom and peace. Let's take a look at some instances of her working toward this end.

Chapter 31 opens with Tara visiting her sister and learning, for the first time, that perhaps Tara isn't the only girl in the family to suffer Shawn's abuse during childhood. This realization teaches Tara that the idea or object before her may not be exactly what it seems. She takes this awareness back to England, where she returns to continue her studies at Cambridge.

At the end of the term, she sees a group of students from her program in the cafeteria and asks to join them. It turns out that one of them has invited the rest to visit him in Rome over the spring holiday. He extends the invitation to Tara as well. She accepts.

While walking through Rome, Tara is struck by how differently she views the ubiquitous historic buildings compared with the other students. "They gave life to the ancient architecture by making it the backdrop of their discourse, by refusing to worship at its altar as if it were a dead thing," she writes.

Until this moment, Tara has almost always viewed the world beyond Buck's Peak as separate from her—a thing requiring a conscious decision for engagement. Here, though, Tara sees that she can learn *while living in her new life*. The new life can *be* her, not just call to her. She stands before a piece of art, Caravaggio's *Judith Beheading Holofernes*, and no longer sees it first from the viewpoint of a person raised on Buck's Peak (as she had when she first encountered the image in an art class textbook years before). This second time, in Rome, Tara's past is beginning to settle into its proper place. Now, she sees the art and lives fully within her current appreciation of and curiosity about it.

"I don't know what caused the transformation," she writes, "why suddenly I could engage with the great thinkers of the past, rather than revere them to the point of muteness … I could admire the past without being silenced by it."

This becomes a crucial step in Tara's eventual ability to consider and acknowledge her past without being silenced by its ongoing presence.

Tara then revisits the writings of Joseph Smith and Brigham Young, the founders and fathers of the Mormon faith. On the mountain, she read their words from the framework of a disciple. Now, she reads them from within a new framework. She's learned how to think critically and apply this to the principles contained in the writings (e.g. polygamy). Tara admits that considering the men's words in this way "felt like a radical act." It likely would for anyone who sets aside blind devotion and instead assesses a religious writing on its own merits. Devotion or religious adherence can wash away a multitude of doctrinal sins. Tara has learned this and now begins to place the Mormon doctrines into a slot in their proper place of her expanded knowledge base.

A third step on Tara's journey to set her past in its place comes when her parents visit her at school. Her dad "testifies" and offers Tara a "priestly blessing." This is an opportunity for Tara to state her allegiance to the truth of her dad's words and his assessment of her as sinful, wayward, etc. Everything Tara has worked through to this point—admitting aloud the abuse she suffered at the hands of Shawn, tentatively walking herself into a classroom and seeking to learn, building relationships with others outside the mountain and their faith community—will be renounced if Tara puts herself under her dad's authority and "truth" again. If she accepts his priestly blessing, she'll be accepting her dad and his ways anew. She will return to the mountain and that life.

Her dad warns Tara that disaster is coming for her, that she'll call out to God in the midst of it but only he—her dad—will respond. He again offers her the opportunity to take his priestly blessing.

"…in that moment, I knew I could not choose it for myself," she writes. "Everything I had worked for, all my years of study, had been to purchase for myself this one privilege: to see and experience more truths than those given to me by my father, and to use those truths to construct my own mind. I had come to believe that the ability to evaluate many ideas, many histories, many points of view, was at the heart of what it means to self-create. If I yielded now, I would lose more than an argument. I would lose custody of my own mind. This was the price I was being asked to pay, I understood that now. What my father wanted to cast from me wasn't a demon: it was me."

Tara tells her dad that she loves him, but she cannot accept his priestly blessing. Her parents pack their things and leave her room.

There will come a time when your new knowledge will be enough to arm you with wisdom. And that wisdom's power will equip you to stand strong in what you know to be true—even when the most powerful forces of your past demand that you return.

The outcome of Tara's decision is revealed a few pages later when she tells of revisiting Buck's Peak. Her feelings about being on the mountain, in her childhood home, have completely shifted. In all her previous visits, Tara fought an inner battle. She wondered whether she was doing the right thing, and she tried to find ways to still be accepted and loved on the mountain even though she was growing into a woman that it did not allow. Each time she returned, she let it harm her in an effort to fit back into it. This time, though, coming after she has refused her father's priestly blessing and stood firm in her newfound knowledge, is different.

Now, Tara can see that the sacrifice required to live inside her past doesn't merit the effort. Life on the mountain has presented her with only conflict, difficulty, harm, and uncertainty.

She enters her mother's kitchen to find the woman sliding biscuits into the oven. Tara looks around and considers whether there is anything in the house she really needs. Only one thing comes to mind: her journals. Tara climbs the stairs, retrieves them, and puts them in her car. Her mother sees this and gets her father, who "…gave me a stiff hug and said, 'I love you, you know that?'" Tara responds, "I do. That has never been the issue."

Tara writes that those are the last words she has spoken to her father.

As Tara grew, she began to question, "…if the first shape a person takes is their only true shape." By reading Mary Wollstonecraft, John Stuart Mill, Thomas Hobbes, Socrates and more, Tara learned that thinking and being can mature into a new shape, and then another new shape, and then yet another new shape. As Maya Angelou stated, "I did then what I knew how to do. Now that I know better, I do better."

Tara learned she, too, could come into a knowing and doing better. Now she acknowledges all of the guilt with which she's wrestled for years—guilt over leaving, over what she did or did not do in response to so many situations and people. "Guilt is the fear of one's own wretchedness," she finally learns. "It has nothing to do with other people." When Tara learns that to grow and change isn't wretched, her guilt disappears.

A final important step in Tara setting her past into its proper place is this: reclaiming the part of her past she still wished to own. For her entire life, Tara has allowed her father to tell the story of who and what she is. Once Tara gains a proper understanding of her past, she returns to the mountain and claims a relationship and presence in the places that hold value and space for the person she has become. The family members who will allow Tara to be an educated, truthful, mature woman are those with whom she reclaims a relationship.

Is there something in your old space that holds value for and acceptance of today's you? Have you relinquished something that you should have grasped? Consider returning for what is worthy to you, and taking it in hands that a wise mind now extends.

CONCLUSION

Tara Westover's brave revelation of her life story provides us with wisdom and illustration of key principles for growing past our own limiting boundaries. By reading her journey from ignorant to educated, we see how choices create outcomes, that when our present costs too much we will seek a new situation, that ignorance allows abuse, that our perception changes when our input changes, that age-old authority isn't always the wisest, that failing in the growth space will tempt us back toward the familiar, that our old ways may hinder us in the new space, that we'll likely lie to ourselves rather than let truth grow us, and that setting our past into its proper place brings freedom.

Growing beyond a limited existence is a hard task. Tara did it. She accomplished it because, through every obstacle and tough circumstance, she *kept choosing* to do it.

So can you.

GIFT:
GUIDED CHALLENGE

Now it's your turn to journal like Tara!

Now is the time to implement all that you have learned in this summary towards your life and professional goals! We know the overwhelming feeling of grappling with the new wealth of information you now carry ... analyzing it, compartmentalizing it, and then applying it. So, we went ahead and formulated a **Guided Challenge to gradually ease you into massive action.** In the Guided Journaling Challenge, you will:

- Consider How You Can Personally Apply Each of the 9 "Educated" Principles

- Develop a Habit of Journaling About Your Day

- Explore a Subject of Fascination For You

Think of the **Guided Challenge as the last excuse on your shelf.** After simply reading the challenge, you simply have no excuses holding you back from implementing the insights of this book to your life.

You can download the Guided Challenge by following the web address: https://www.exegrowth.com/pdfguide-e-20

You can also follow the steps below to instantly access your exclusive Guided Challenge:

1. **Open** your smart phone's camera application

2. **Aim** your phone's camera **and focus on** the QR Code below

3. **Click** the link that pops up on the top side of your screen

If you downloaded *Power Insights* at the start of the summary check your inbox, the Guided Challenge awaits you.

Our team at Executive**Growth** cannot thank you enough for believing in our work and trusting us to deliver the wisdom within *Educated: A Memoir* directly to you.

The mission of our team is to elevate the quality and productivity of our readers' personal and professional lives by providing clear, entertaining, and impactful summaries of timeless works.

If you feel that we have done right by our mission, please leave a review on Amazon by following the web address http://bit.ly/egreview. Your review will go a long way for our growing company.

If you do not feel we met our mission or can improve in any facet of our summary books, we would also love to hear from you too! We are always trying to make our quality better and your feedback is pivotal in the process — don't hold back any punches; we have thick skin. Please leave your feedback by following the web address http://www.exegrowth.com/feedback.

We hold you in the highest regard for investing in yourself! We are committed to staying your companions in this exciting yet challenging journey of personal growth. **Let's go and let's grow!**

Links:
Educated: A Memoir **Full Book:** https://www.amazon.com/
    Educated-Memoir-Tara-Westover/dp/0399590501/
Guided Challenge: https://www.exegrowth.com/pdfguide-e-20
Amazon Review: http://bit.ly/egreview
Executive Growth Feedback: http://exegrowth.com/feedback

NOTES:
CAPTURE YOUR THOUGHTS

_____

_____

_____

_____

_____

_____

_____

_____

_____

_____

_____

_____

_____

_____

_____

_____

_____

_____